Beatlemania
(*and other real tales*)

Beatlemania
(and other real tales)

Manuel Renaud

Beatlemania (and other real tales)
by Manuel Renaud

Author's Note

I would like to thank James Goddard for his precious help and for the opportunity he offered me by publishing this book.

First published in 2019 by
Leaky Boot Press
http://www.leakyboot.com

Copyright © 2019 Manuel Renaud
All rights reserved

No part of this book may be reproduced or transmitted in any form or by any means, electronic, mechanical, photocopying, recording, or otherwise, without prior written permission of the author.

ISBN: 978-1-909849-81-5

Contents

Chapter one
Poems on a windshield

A deep song	11
Beatlemania	12
Off-season	13
Green	14
Cloud	15
The Lamb	16
After the storm	18
Zeppelin	19
The complete works of Arthur Rimbaud	21
Tales from summer days	22
You and I	24
The Faun and the Minstrel	25
Free Jump	27
Island	28
Laundry room and garden	29
Wyatt	30
The *Jardin des plantes*	*32*
Wonder	33
An Autumn's tale (*one season episode one*)	34
Tencc	36
Adagietto	37
Quadrophenia	38
Dinard	39
The fab one	41

Chapter two
In the open country

Short Poem	45
Tales from the Château	46

Lullaby	48
Peter	49
Last bad weather	51
Young	52
Freeze frame	53
Pet sounds	55
My only one	57
The Hotel	59
In Love	62
A trip to India	63
Heart	65
Bend on the run	66
London	68
White	69
An autumn's tale (*one season episode two*)	70
Ray	72
The Piano	74
John Lennon's music	76
October	77
In rock	78
At dawn	80
Station to station	81

Chapter three
The lift and the road

He's there	85
More and more	87
The way	89
Tales from Stratocaster	91
The veranda	93
McCartney	94
Prayer	96
Tales from rainy days	97
November	99
A night at the opera	101
Above the garden (*in the diaphanous hours*)	102
Free	103
The pebble	104
A day in the life of John Lennon	106

The gardens of the Alhambra	108
It's five o'clock	109
An autumn's tale (*one season episode three*)	110
An Englishman	111
December	112
Hard day's clouds	113
It's falling	115
Abba	117
Gleam	119
The complete works of The Beatles	120

Chapter one

Poems on a windshield

A deep song

A deep song
Beyond
The father's song
And grandfathers'
The ancients' song
They will be reborn
The song of the stars

Beatlemania

A horse in New york
Running along the limo
8 mm camera
Mounties
N.Y. Long avenues
The four boys behind the windows
Watching the world a-changing
All is going so fast
The big car's parking by the pavement
Beatlemania
One can only see
The animal's chest
And the top of its legs
Children rushing around
Finally catching up with them
Screams, laughs, faces
The film and its images
Beatlemania
The Big Apple in black and white
The riders
Teenage sky
Will sing
Beatlemania

Off-season

The beach lies down
Till the end of fall
The dirt road doesn't meet anyone
The traveler between two silences
Continues his way under a thin rain
Without reason
His bundle's swaying
To the slow rhythm of his steps
He doesn't know what he's going through
He doesn't care, he's not there
He's walking, empty pockets
He only has a few wrinkles
He's coming from afar
One can see that
At the end of months
The very end of years
He's home everywhere
Simply going by
Without waiting for the horizon
Off-season

Green

Everything's green over there
The river, the foliages
The sky turns to blue
Early in the morning
At fresh dawns
Fishermen on the banks
Feet in the mud
It's been raining at night
The old tan leather
And the unshaven mugs
Bayou is ageless
The rock smells the soil
After the storm
Hicks' stories
Full of witches and spells
And full of dancing girls
Her bare feet in the grass
Their moving shadows
In the night of camp fires
Flames in their eyes
In their laughters
Promises never kept
For another blues
Another song
Under a yellow moon
For all that green around
And this water so clear

Cloud

Silence of the sky
Dumb blue upon our heads
Upon our lowered eyes
Blindness of the heart
Eyes in the mist
Uproot the verbs
Words of exile
Fake their truths
Bargain ignorance
Delude themselves, lost
In deaf gossips
Horizontal
Sanctuary in the clouds
Cloud

The Lamb

I'm mowing the lawn
Around 5 P.M
In the shade of the house
It's still warm out there
A flock of ewes
Is going by
On the way below
Along the fence
Late, clumsy
A lost lamb
Comes in through the half open gate
He's there in the cut grass
Frightened, he's looking around
He doesn't see the broad path
Stony, dusty
He's white on green
By late afternoon
The lawn will surely wait
I'm sitting on a bench
Taking him in my arms
That's where he falls asleep
Follow him in siesta
His head on my knees
His eyes are closed
I have a so strange dream
Inhabited by absurd characters
In an unknown town
In a long night

The shepherd wakes me up
His lamb lost and found
After the bend over there
The path is wide
It leads to a village
Another village
It's quite late to mow
I'll finish tomorrow

After the storm

Only silence remains
The scent of the wet grass
And dancing joyful children
Their clothes already stained
Only the taste of rain remains
On the leaves of the trees

Zeppelin

A round trip
London. N.Y. London
A tea room
Under the airship
And the Atlantic Ocean
And the clouds
The radio plays a popular tune
A rhythmical music
Which makes passengers want to dance
Want to smile
She wants to smile
That very passenger
A nice Lady
A flapper girl
In that journey time
Always the ocean
It's raining on the fabric skin
The Zeppelin's shivering
It's flying through the wind
By the window
Far westward
It meets the night
Noiseless
This suffragette's speaking so loud
And her look is clear
And her laugh's lulling me
I no longer listen to her words
I'm looking at her mouth

At her summer eyes
At her hands which jazz
Therefore I'm talking
Am I the one who make her so joyful…?
I don't really know
Maybe the Champagne
Conversation of bodies
Sensual and silent
She's heading for California
To meet up with her husband
The Zeppelin's capsizing
For a while
She wishes me "goodnight!
Have a nice sojourn in N.Y City!
See you soon maybe
In another life
At a Led Zeppelin gig!"
Roaring seventies

The complete works of Arthur Rimbaud

In the backpack
Between two stations
A voice saying his name
I can hear Arthur Rimbaud
How heavy those pages
Tube without stop
However I'll get off
On the platform, images
On the walls, the poems
Sparks on the tracks
Sleeper in the battle
Then corridors lead me away
Infiltrations
Autumn draughts
I'm reading and shivering
It's been raining all season long
An underground river
A boat for Verlaine
Vowels in a row
Colours to the exit
Just a few more steps
Walking words don't speak it
Last sentences for infinity
The sky is here, blue, beautiful
The complete works of Arthur Rimbaud

Tales from summer days

I was breathing underwater
Until the ocean deeps
Silent landscapes
Sea bottom
Valleys, mountains
My eyes in the sleeve
My heart in the picture
The sea music
The still journey
Eyes closed
Sound as only luggage
Words, submarine poems
To speak the light
So far from the sky
So far from the sun
A tale from wisdom and sand
Great sound frescoes
Electric bas-reliefs
Grace between the notes
Intuition of beauty
The liquid veil
On my child's skin
The double album
Tales from summer days
Fleeting reflections
Of truth and peace
The garden of seaweeds and corals
Inspiration

Expiration
Love without breathing
Snatches of eternity
Vibrations
Music
Ils sont du soleil

You and I

You and I
Like two strangers in this world
Under the same sun
A well round earth
Just for you and me

You and I
Like two "faraways" kissing
In the same silence
The same traces
Which remain in you and me

All of our todays
All that present
Each minute of our lives
Continues its way
Somehow

You and me
Like two memories in the heart
Not the same sun anymore
The same happiness
It was you and me

The Faun and the Minstrel

The faun in the morning
In the freshness of woods
Is raising his flute
Invisible in the coppices
He's playing for the nymphs
Hidden under the leaves
Scared, shy
In those days
A minstrel passing through
His ears wide open
Heard that music
Which enchanted his mind
And overwhelmed his heart
As the evening came
With his companions
Strolling players, musicians
In the court of the Lord
He gracefully replayed
That so delicate tune
He sang so many tales
Legends and dreams
The whole gallery
Became a place of mysteries
His music exhilarated
This noble assembly
Carried away in spite of itself
By the faun's magic
The minstrel bowed to the audience

His melody still floating away
In their smiles and in their eyes
The faun fell asleep
In the night under a tree
His flute by his side

Free Jump

Free jump
Free parachute
From up there
All that sky
All that wind in the wings
Widely spread
Like generous arms
Hug that happy man
Who's coming back cleaned up
Washed out from the mud of stars
Big as an ocean
Which'd within flow away

Island

I'll go on that island
With a crimson sun
Red in the sky
And this starless night
Deserted hut
An old Bible gone black
On a rickety table
A makeshift palace
For a so wretched monarch
In the court of the King of brambles
A Temple in the jungle
Slowly engulfed
By all this wild green
And on its wall of glory
So many unknown words
Still vestiges
Of those lost prayers
A few mildewed pages
Faded illuminations
I'll re-board to my boat
Empty-handed with no treasure
And I'll row, thoughtful
My eyes on that picture
On this drawn star
Sleeve of secrets
Only revealed by sounds

Laundry room and garden

The moon's so beautiful in the clouds
It's night time in the garden
The laundry room's asleep
I'm listening to the silence of the stars
A music begins
Like a mysterious dream
Swaying in the wind of my childhood
Its fancy wings
Fly me to tomorrow morning
A taste of sun keeps coming back to me
A new colour
In this mysterious song
In the garden
In the laundry room
A new day
All is in blossom

Wyatt

Robert in the field
Is picking up flowers
Ocean stones
Those of the bottom
His hat of sun
His straw hat
His underwater piano
With a wheelchair
He flies across the sky
His voice in the clouds
At tea time
Robert in the garden
Hoeing and watering
Vegetables in a row
On the keyboard
A plant poem
The gardener's hands
In the soil of sounds
It's Canterbury
On the island over there
He will stand dancing
Despite sadness
The depth of hidden words
This gracious melancholy
This sweet irony
The British rain
The downpour's passenger
Robert in the canopy

Is looking at the drops
They're crying for him
Yet he's smiling
It's summertime
In Canterbury

The *Jardin des plantes*

It rains on the *Jardin des plantes*
Its wet benches where nobody sits
Its soaked paths and its joyless puddles
Its grey, slow and voiceless shadows
It rains on the sun of past days
Botany is powerless
A sad rain almost insolent
Heavily falling on my thoughts
And all its drops like so much tears
Like sorrow for all these flowers
It's now raining on happiness
And water washes out its colours
Its fingers stubbornly striving
To smear it, to wipe it out
It's even raining on my memories
Like a drizzle on the pictures
A cold fog on the faces
The lapping is meaningless
And its silence is a downpour
In this time I'm going through
My heart flooded

Wonder

Sweet as this summer of
Lush songs
In the garden of wonders
Words full of flowers
Of joy and love
His look turned towards the ones he loves
Towards the world around
Yes… His look
Gifts for the heart
Suns for the ears
Stars, stars again
In his smile, his voice
Useful vibrations
Despite the bottomless well
Of ignorance and certainties
His words of consciousness
Of sharing
I can recall
Sweet as this summer of
Happiness in the garden
Wonders
This masterpiece
I'm listening to
Limitless, generous
So human
Simply human
I love you

An Autumn's tale (*one season episode one*)

THE CHARMING PRINCE

It's raining on the station
It's raining on the square
The Charming Prince
His elbows leant on the bar
Unable to stand still
Had drunk his last cup of coffee
The waiter's already setting the chairs
Soon the brasserie will be closed
It's already past midnight
One after another
The streets stop talking
A badly parked pumpkin
Tomorrow will be fined
The Charming Prince just realized
That Cinderella won't come
Cinderella won't come no more
Outside in the rain
He's walking back and forth
The Charming Prince
What does he say to himself…?
He doesn't know it
In his Palace already far too big
He's only a wandering shadow
On the ground, left there
A glass slipper

Cinderella won't come
And her absence like glasspaper
Will scratch... his heart

Tencc

This very song
Was for you
This very summer
Grains of gold dust
In your oceanlike pupils
Yet it was saying
"I'm not in love"
A bit cynical
Almost ironic
With this so British distance
This sounding modesty
Contradicted the words
The melody
The harmony
Really loved you
It was the message
That I didn't dare
It was there
In this very song
Sometimes I can hear
This very song
It's our secret
But... Of course
You know it

Adagietto

This slow movement
Of my hands on your skin
Only the feeling
That gesture is a C
The caress of that chord
Which still for so long
In my heart will sound
Until silence… so far beyond
Until this infinite tenderness
This wordless song of love
The embrace of the Adagietto
The melodic line of your lips
That violins softly whisper
Those dumb sentences raising
These sounds getting through all the walls
Those frozen walls of our silences
These frostbitten lands of our distances
My orchestra's good and beautiful friends
Like one heart, one tempo
All your bows for just an arrow
The embrace of the Adagietto
Harmony, there laid
That warm breath on your eyelids
Like this very first kiss
Notes alive taking flesh
Sun, violas and cellos
Basses, last pizzicato
The embrace of the Adagietto

Quadrophenia

In the rear-view mirrors
The edge of the cliff
The one of Dover, the English one
The beach, the sand and the scooter
Last sunday of july
Mods and rockers fraternize
The war's no longer obligatory
Songs in the sky
Birds of youth
Jubilant crowds
Rebels' stories
In the rear-view mirror
The working class
Rock and misery
Still a double album
Colourless pictures
This rough black and white
An unhappy kid
years of the other century
That's "Gare de l'Est" (Paris)
The poem's still fluttering about
Some riffs in the tube
Pieces of sentences in the bus
Tonight I won't get out of it…!
I'll listen to Quadrophenia once again

Dinard

Dinard
She's so alone, no one to hold her hand
It's summer time, she's walking on the strand
She's wandering, how could she understand?

Dinard
Her lovely souvenirs are on the run
Echoes of laughter, moments of fun
Behind her shades her eyes are numb.
Another day
Another dance
Another romance
Another tune she wansta play
Another moonshine on the bay
Her phono cries and goes astray
Her song is over
She's waiting for another tide so she can sail away

Dinard
In her dress tonight, she's looking fine
She's been waiting for him until nine
She hears her favorite melody line
Another day
Another dance
Another romance
Another tune she wansta play
Another moonshine on the bay
Her phono cries and goes astray
She hides her tears and smile away
She's waiting for another tide so she can sail away

Dinard
Here comes the sunshine in her eyes
A really dizzy wind blows inside
Her heart is open wide
She's dancing in the sky
Her new love is so high
In the air she can fly.

Dinard
Through the clouds they're loving again
Morning mist they walk hand in hand
Another tide, another day
But in the end… for such a love
There is no end.

The fab one

Olympia
Unvarnished nostalgia
I let my beautiful memories
Coming
Simple tears with them
This deep vibration
Still intact
Old British lads
And Ringo
Magical wands
I didn't dream
I went with him
Like always
Like before
Now
My Liverpool fellow's
Universal smile

Chapter two

In the open country

Short Poem

Short poem
St Martin Canal
Within an ace of the lock
In your bag the thin fabric
On your heart
My warm palms
Bobo' time
Is at the station
The sun is hurting
Stupid like my words
So clumsy

Tales from the Château

It's summertime in the Château
And Lady Jane is getting bored
The Count is hunting
He's riding in the sun
Since early in the morning
Yet she's so beautiful
And life is so sweet
In Touraine
Despite all the bouquets
The armfuls of flowers
The great feasts, the balls
Lady Jane is fretting
And secretly crying
She's waiting for this storm
This rain on her skin
Thunder in the sky
A wind to make stones rolling along
In the paths of the park.
A so pleasant neighbour
A handsome English Lord
Courteous and charming
With a weird look
With a strange smile
Filled with shadows and fire
Deeply moved Lady Jane.
"Please allow me to introduce myself
I'm poet and musician
In my spare time

I'm known as a man of taste
And fortune smiled on me
I'm writing a few songs too
I know
It's only rock'n'roll
Hope you'll like them!"
Woman of duty, intuitive
Despite her attraction
She offered all her sympathy to him
She'll listen to him with pleasure
But she had guessed
Despite her fascination
Who he really was
And one surely knows
That he can't really take in with women
He couldn't get no satisfaction.

Lullaby

Little girl of shadows
Humming this lullaby
La, la, la, la, goodbye
Sweet and sad "chanson"
Chatting with her dolls
Secret, inner sentences
Whispered to the ears
Little girl of silences
Singing nursery rhymes
Dancing and nodding
Light innocence
Little girls of tears
Getting through the rain
How she grew up…!
Getting through the flames
Little girl of heart
Lulling mother
Loving mother
Little girls of weeps
La, la, la, la, strumming
This simple melody
The sun tells you so
Just a few notes

Peter

In the real world
I stopped dreaming
In the dreams of others
In the words of others
In the songs of others
You don't know me
Anonymous suburbanite
I don't blame you
You're not guilty
I loved you like a son
Who was waiting in vain
For this sentence forever fell silent
"I'm proud of you"
I'm proud of myself
Without conceit
Without complacency
In working and doubts
I put away all your records
I don't listen to them anymore
They are here in my head
In my heart
I'm not that pupil any more
Waiting for the good mark
The reassuring look
Of the wise and fair master
In the real world
That I had never known
I met you

As you are
A great artist
I'm going away Peter
All my heroes are dead
All those tutelary figures
Will never acknowledge me
They only existed to survive
I'm living now
They're within their place
I'm within mine
My dreams belong to me at last

Last bad weather

Last bad weather
And then that peace
In a summer sky
This fulfilled silence
Its stillness
Few words in the clouds
Some thoughts
To love
As far as all these landscapes
Those journeys

Young

Like the old Young
Lumberjack, shirt
Jacket, trapper
Patched blue jeans
His harp, his 'Martin'
In North Ontario
The pick-up, the great forests
The wind in his guitar
Blowing to California
His songs of anger
Closeness of the words
Hidden pains
In the course of a ballad
Of a whispered folk-song
Murmured
After the gold rush
Precious melodies
On the beach, the loner
Still
An impression of *déjà vu*
Already heard
Until the heart of trees
On the road
The walker
Will take his coffee
In the next town
And will cross the look
Of that fancied girl
He has always dreamt of

Freeze frame

Villas by the seaside
Beach tents blue and white
All is sunday, all is slow
On the horizon, seaside resort
A garden chair near the sky
The little flat like a boat
The bow of the balcony in the sun
Over there sailships sliding on the waves
Freeze frame
My thoughts are flying till the roofs
Where the seagulls are nattering
Where time's softly stopping
Its open wings
Its light feathers under my fingers
Freeze frame
Doughnuts for the evening
Italian icecreams outside
So much smiles in her look
It's happiness passing by
Why not...?
Freeze frame
She's laughing at my childlike jokes
We're alone in the landscape
I can hear her crystalline sentences
The film in the film
We're walking on the sand
Freeze frame
She's taking my arm

So tender and dreamy
Knowing glances of old children
The end of the movie can wait
In that very moment, she's taking my hand
Freeze frame

Pet sounds

It should be a postcard
In a cardboard box of memories
Images come to life
The wind is rising
California is back
With its girls in the sun
Its hawaian shirts
Its big beaches
Its nice waves
Summer stopped here
On the old pictures
Tanned guys
Sweet songs
Forever
Happy teenage time
Didn't want to get old
Peter Pan's still surfing
Over there in the mirror
Years of dreams
A vanilla and strawberry taste
For those times of carefreeness
It should be a postcard
The beach is deserted
Early in the morning
A guy is walking his dog
Pacific is waking up
A running girl
Is still listening on headphones

To her parents' songs
"Pet sounds"

My only one

I know the wounds
The bites right through the heart
The relieving glances
Brushing happiness
I know the angers
Storm of words
The fleeting suns
Of your hands on my skin
O my love, my love
My only one
My lovely one
I know the way
In the night to the station
That fog for tomorrow
Like a train losing its way
I know the pains
The dialogues of the deaf
The perfumes of your flowers
The backs and the forths
You know my wanders
Promises in the wind
You know my silences
Their colours within
I know the grief
That old friend of mine
The nightmares in the mornings
Still another day
I know the reproaches

Time of illusions
Time of deceptions
Despite the summer sky
It's winter time I'm passing through
Despite the smiles of the whole world
A rain of tears that I'm shedding
Again and again
I surely know that your life
Will embrace me
Prevent the sun going out
Despite the coldness
Despite the grey
O my love, my love
My only one

The Hotel

It was a long time ago
In the middle of nowhere
I was traveling then
In a desert or somewhere else
Right in the blazing sunshine
Maybe Nevada
Or California
Anyway, far from the sea
A story full of cliches
Watched and watched again
In all those movies
These backs of beyond
Along the highway
And this gas station
For that nth full tank
Towards somewhere
Where it will be better
It is eventually hoped
Without believing too much
All was there
The bar, the ventilator
The waitress's boredom
"May I take your order?"
And this hairy guy
Hirsute
His lowered eyes
Lost in his thoughts
Indifferent, distant

His beer already lukewarm
In front of him on the table
His tatooed arms
Hands flat
It looked like he was praying
And then...
He turned his head
Needed to talk undoubtedly
A weird story
Bit by bit, disjointed
He had just taken a walk
A random walk without compass
He just escaped
At least that's what I understood
A convict on the run...?
It was far worse than that...!
Some time ago
A total eclipse
The night in broad daylight
During minutes
He was gone at last
Nothing held him back
This time
He turned back
A last time
Free on the road
Before him
Without really knowing why
In the distance
The neons of the hotel
Were lighting that very moment
He saw the letters
Taken away one after the other
It was already past
Hotel California
At dawn
This first dawn

The music stopped
An eagle in the blue
In the blue sky
Its wings on the horizon
Then he smiled at me
He wanted to pay for me
He insisted
He was tired
He seemed to be happy
We drove the highway together
Looking at life
Living it too
Talking about tomorrow
Just talking

In Love

I just wanna tell you that
I will always love you and
I will fly
You and I in the sky of Love
We'll fly
Our tears are rolling
They won't dry
Our eyes are open
Open wide
In the light of Love they're shining

I just wanna tell you that
It's time for our loving to be
Life is gonna love you and me
We're gonna change
Gonna heal inside
Gonna feel that peace is coming

I just wanna tell you that
I'm so in love with you
I'm so in love it's true
I just wanna love you, wanna love you
Every single day
I just wanna love you every day

A trip to India

The gardener and his flowers
His rubber boots
In the English grass
His garden gnomes
New friends of loneliness
Under a rainy sky
A new freedom
A bit bitter
His long chants
Shrouded in the fog
Slightly naive prayers
A trip to India
Pop mantras
The dream was over
A new page
A new chapter
Time went by
Like things and human beings
That one had loved so much
A new decade
Meditative hours
Back to back
The father and the son
Are silently talking to each other
Flesh against flesh
At peace together again at last
The lost and renewed ties
Pierced by love

By tenderness
Forgiveness of wandering years
I'm giving you that triple album
You're giving me a smile
A peaceful look
The garden's blooming again
Generously
The kitchen garden's offering us
Its greens

Heart

At the end of those images
Almost forgotten
Almost wiped out
Faceless shadows
More and more distant
Lost, evaporated
Almost vanished
Towards that cloudy sky
Somewhere else taken away
Night words
Making a poem
They kiss each other
They love each other
They make life
It makes rain so often
It makes sun sometimes
It makes sky I think
It makes smiles, it makes wind
It makes so many years
It's still day
It makes multicoloured silences
It makes hummings and chants
It makes time, moments
It makes beaches and landscapes
It makes first shore
Now it makes dawn
Despite grief and tears
It makes light
It makes feelings

Bend on the run

Anywhere
Hope
Somewhere else
After the street corner
In another district
Other faces
New friends
Far from town
From hot summer
From boredom
In a tinkered motor
With a stranded girl
On the road
Once again
The old cliches
The seats in the back
The convertible
On the run to nowhere
To get out of the hole
The hole in the head
The hole in the heart
Never been in New Jersey
This rough voice
Hoarse
Screaming ghost
Of the American dream
Which haunts his nights
Urban nightmares

The myth is born again
In fits and starts
The world has grown older
A thick fog
Some upheavals
Poets remain silent
I'm wrong
They're still speaking
But the uproar's too strong
One can't hear them anymore
Divas are selling silence and wind
In the streets full of memories

London

The ferry, my old banger
The sun rises on the left
In England
I watch straight ahead
It's July in your eyes
London's happy in summer
Its blue is island "bleu"
Streets and buses upside down
Adventurous crossroads
Ordinary's full of love
Those light-minutes
At the speed of traffic jams
The road atlas on your knees
Losing its way but it don't care
Yes..! We're a-livin' that great
When life's buzzing
With starry smiles
We've done so well to go there
To kiss
Those very days in the heart of "Londres"

White

It was the time of the White Album
Its black vinyl an ocean
Of always multicoloured waves
My heart in the sounding tides
It was the time of the great treasures
Open coffins full of guitars
Full of so hyped songs
For the children's eyes
For the ears I used to have
Which only listened to happiness
Flames for imagination
Torrents of light
It was the time of the colours
I do remember it now
It was the time of the White Album

An autumn's tale (*one season episode two*)

CINDERELLA

It's evening time in town
The landau has arrived
It's waiting before her gate
Whites horses to take her away
His last message told her:
"Rendezvous at the brasserie
Cinderella
Before midnight,
I'll wait there for you
The Prince, my Darling dear"
And rain's making the journey
Cinderella's crying, she doesn't know anymore
Is it still a sweet mirage…?
Cinderella alone is feeling lost
And the coachman can't hear her
"Please turn back!
Please stop here!
Right on this square, at the crossroad!
The Charming Prince is not for me
He's too much Prince
Too much Charming!
He loves me
I love him
I can't realize
Nothing I know about feelings."
Cinderella's walking in the night

She won't go to the rendezvous
Her tears are falling, it's midnight
The streets are black
The streets are blurred
Cinderella knows it's over.

Ray

Keep off the grass
We don't care
The weather's fine up there
And the old Ray
Is coming along
In the afternoon
The sunny rock
Carefree
This very present
Light, volatile
Without the clouds
Of the day after tomorrow
The little Kings
In their youth
The old world
As old as ever
Seemed to slowly fade away
It was waiting for its time to come
Simply
Crouching in the grass
It let things go
It'd come back to work things out
We surely could dream
Of freedom and peace
The moneymakers' factories
Were still running so well
Meantime
We didn't really think about it

We wanted to escape
From that discreet nightmare
Flowers and girls
The old Ray's poems
Yet were telling us about it
As the dream was over
The "keep off the grass"
Drowned with smoke bombs
Sleepwalkers, bitter
Our illusions were
Creased papers
In our child's pockets
Back to normalcy
Thank you anyway my dear Ray
It was so fine
Tell me...? Did we love each other...?
Really...?

The Piano

A keystroke
A brushstroke of blue
A keystroke
A brushstroke of red
A keystroke
A brushstroke of green
The tonic chord
Perfect harmony
The voiceless smile
Still notes
Awaiting in line
Patient keyboard
An open door
Curtains and windows
Towards the garden
Towards so many roses
Fingers fumbling about
Pebble after pebble
Tom Thumb
Finds his path
And all the others
Discover the road
Still frightened
Still clumsy
But they already play
Despite the persistent shadow
The old clouds
Full of night

Both your hands
Get together
Sounds are proud to sound
They're all dressing up
For a sunday
Music is on its way
For the feast
The piano in the soul
The piano in the heart
Your old friend
Opens its arms
It's already embracing you
You're at home now

John Lennon's music

My old white turntable stopped
I put the black record into its sleeve
Skinned songs of silence
Like a sky striped with lightnings of childhood
Screams, wounds in his words
Drops of blood on the piano
Yet it was summer under the tree
A summer of wiping the slate clean
He no longer believed in much
An illusion drove out another
Another dream had begun
I tasted these two halves of an apple
The John Lennon's music

October

October in silence
Half-opened shutters
A forgotten scarf
Sweet and light presence
The coffee's flowing on its own
To the bottom of the cup
Ocean under ice
Its black under the red of leaves
October and its spoon
Apricot jam
Leftover in the bottom of the pot
I'll be shopping yesterday
Mornings October themselves
The days follow them
In small steps their hours are drifting
Autumn launch
October shells
Last seasonal suns

In rock

Only one record shop
At "St-Lazare" station (Paris)
France was still variety-like singing
I had seen '68 passing by
I was 10
3 weeks of holidays
I was still playing marbles
It was so far from me
So far above my head
In the clouds of childhood
The talkatives' revolution
They had to change the world
I had to make a choice
Not much money
"L.A Woman" or "In Rock"
The sleeve was ugly
Pretentious
That's what I'm saying today
Never really liked The Doors
Morrisson the smashed up poet
With his tipsy lyrics
Too much dark and obscure
So… "In Rock"
Blackmore's guitar
Without thinking over
Nobody played like that
As simple as that
So… "In Rock"

For a long time
Forever
Undoubtedly

At dawn

Above the trains
Sky between buildings
The sun begins
Platforms in the morning
Misty monologue
Of hurriers to the station
Glances inside
Eyes asleep
Free papers
Faceless cars
The other one in the picture
Invisible, casual almost
It's dawn in the suburb
With its ordinary ways
Its shadows of routine
Little bright heart
Little lights for the street
The day soliloquies
Thoughts clattering
Silence keeps going
Its way to the day
Little steps of love
As dawn's back
The few may I see
It's here

Station to station

An Aladdin's lamp
In each compartment
Smoker and non-smoker
The handsome chameleon
Is walking on the tracks
From station to station
From character to character
A guard
Is checking the tickets
Enigmatic waiter
Of the restaurant car
A spaceship
In the baggage hold
From glance to glance
A solar clown
Is silently crying
Inconsolable
Iggy and Ziggy
The electric duettists
At the next stop
Maybe in the next world
After the hill over there
The Duke and Freddy
Are playing cards
In a private lounge
The train's going away
One can hear it sometimes
When the wind consents

Some evenings
When we close our eyes
We'll certainly have to dance
Let's dance..!
Let's smile...!

Chapter three

The lift and the road

He's there

He's there in the morning
He's living at home
I can see him in the sky
He has the taste of bread
The strength of silence
I smell his perfume
When I'm thirsty, when I'm hungry
If I cry then he's dancing
He's there under the rain
As I'm smiling for a sun
When I'm kidding he's waking up
To say he was only half asleep
A name of a street
A platform of a station
A cafe, a glance
Quickly crossed, quickly unknown
I'm looking at my shadow
In the eyes of a lamp post
In the night, in the light
In the noise of crowds
In this enlightened December
I can see him in the shop windows
In the children's joy
At the foot of the fir
And before the chimney
He's there until the evening
In all the movies, all the pictures
He has always the same face

He's there in the mirror
Between two words
At the end of a sentence
At the end of the drying
I put on off
I'm taking out the warm linen
He's there between the gestures
At the end of the broom
Pieces of fluff
At the end of tears
The sponge will tell me: "no!"
He's all what's left to me
Even if to keep him silent
I'm listening to
"The Song of the Earth"
By Gustav Mahler
He can't hear the far away echo
Of happiness
Just here in my heart

More and more

Both sides of the sun
Are still shining at night
The one of the moonshadow
And its reflection in dawn
It's high tide
Salty waters are back
The coast is a fancy line
Seen from the sky
A blue and white stroke
The foam of waves
And the ocean
A kind of green
For your eyes
For that summer dress
That you're wearing
More and more often
The wind makes you dance
In the pictures
In my head
We were listening to that
Music of pink
In the shade
Clouds to the ceiling
Of your room
Till the evening
I do remember you
More and more
And silence keeps recurring

Once again
Always the same question

The way

It's a way in the mist
I don't know where it's leading to
It leads to you
It's a song in the mist
Which tells you that I love you
Blown by the wind
Near to you
It's a hope in the mist
Which guides me and drags me off
With each step
It's a road in the mist
Lit by my lantern
Little sun which loves you
In the coldness
I'm going back home
With this song
Its words of love for you
It's your glance in the mist
I know it brings me back
Up against you
It's that sun in the mist
This heart which takes me back
I can hear how it beats
For you
In silence and in mist
Under a cloudy sky
I can only hear my steps
And you're here

Its a way under the moon
Little stones one sows
Little candles one lights
For you
I'm getting back home
With this song
Its words of love for you

Tales from Stratocaster

An old Strat in a shop window
"This one's not for sale…!
Nobody could play that guitar…!
It's in a perfect state
But I don't know why
It doesn't sound at all…!
No doubt, it's surely waiting
For its true owner…!"
A lefty Strat
In its old suitcase
"Kinda Arthur's sword…!"
He said with a smile:
"One cast a spell on it…!"
With a wink
I'm trying it anyway
Just to see
The strings actually don't sound
Amplifier on
Guitar plugged
Silence…!
Mystery…!
The next days
I'm talking about it
To one of my pupils
A very gifted little boy
"Would you like to try it
Just for fun…?"
Like in all tales

Chance doesn't exist
Always a happy ending story
With no other explanation
It's a magical time
It was waiting for the kid
The dealer asked no question
Chords came back to life
Under his nimble fingers
Then I asked him:
"Do you know to whom it belonged...?"

The veranda

It's softly raining
It's tenderly raining
On the window panes
Of the veranda
Gleams of June
At the end of the sheets
The bolster then the pillow
Somewhere a summer dress
Little rag fallen on the ground
Left out in the night
The murmur of a fabric
Offered by your voiceless eyes
A glance towards infinity
You're sleeping without haste
Right in the morning's heart
Nothing important, nothing bothersome
The sky's discreet as the storm breaks
You're smiling in your sleep
In your dreams of rain
In the day, in the shelter
Soon the sun
It will wait for you
It knows your peaceful breath
Modesty of a little kiss
On your cheek, in the veranda

McCartney

About fifteen minutes
To get back home
The gate, the path, my house
The wisteria its sweet perfume
I was in the kitchen already
Threw my heavy satchel aside
Books, exercise books on the table
And the whole world was a-stopping
I was listening to McCartney
Right in the dining-room
I was given a few chords
To colour the world
Those were the ordinary days
Long years of childhood
My life was a school life
I was innocence only
McCartney was smiling in the sun
After school had begun
The biggest gig of all
My only guitar was a broom
For fancy songs
Music was humming her colours
I loved her in silence
Happiness's so simple
When it is in childhood
McCartney was smiling in the sun
Then one day my parents
Offered me a guitar, a real one

On wednesdays
I was singing in English
In my laundry room for real
Then I was McCartney
In such a nice dream
Music fulfilled my life

Prayer

Let's hope that dawn
Opens its arms of sky
Offers its hands of sun
Let's hope that the air
Vibrates to wings and leaves
Let's hope that water
Quenches that very morning
And fills your flask
Let's hope that silence
Welcomes the light
The grace of a piece of bread
And the honey of hope
Let's hope that your lantern
Lights your doubts a bit
And each of your steps
And each of your nights
Let's hope that on the horizon
After so many journeys
The roof of your house
Its opened windows
The door of your heart

Tales from rainy days

It rains on the old mountain path
The summit in the clouds
Water's softly streaming down
A pale sun in the autumn mists
The old man and his lantern
His big hood his only shelter
Silently crossing
Slowly
The last mystery
Bend after bend
Stones under his feet
Roots sprung up from the earth
And the trees are draining
They're splashing about in the wind
Their bare branches
Seem to pray
A prayer for the traveler
The rain song
The night is about to come
The road still very long
He'll take a rest
And then a new dawn will come
A new rainy tomorrow
And so many others
The mountain is so high
The slope is so stiff
Nobody's ever seen him again
And no one knows if up there

He's found what he was looking for
The mountain is still here
With its aimless path

November

Slowly
Days November themselves
They're dressing warmly
Without being surprised
By the cold mornings
Ad Libitum calendar days
They're all looking alike
Colourless noria
Some pale greys
Greens and yellows
A bit of orange colours
The tree in the yard
Is still counting its leaves
It's so sleepy
Despite the wind, it yawns
It's dropping its branches
Vertical sleeper
Boyfriend become great friend
I also November myself
Inextricable glacis
Bramble bushes till I bleed
Stinging regrets
Scrape the hours
And all the minutes
The poem Novembers itself
Its hesitating words
Distraught images
Crossed-out, started again

The dead leaves of the text
Its sentences of rain
And the shadow of wind
Laconic draught
Life Novembers itself
Heart silences itself
Beat after beat
Days November themselves
Slowly

A night at the opera

We're going to laugh
We're going to dance
We're going to have fun
At the unmasked ball
Of the Queen of dreams
The ceiling is a summer sky
Lit by torches
The fancy-dressed guests
So many starry chandeliers
To illuminate the dance floor
Fire-eaters
Magicians
Jugglers
The orchestra is invisible
It's silently playing
All the music
We can hear through the heart
The song of the world
At the planetary ball
Of the Queen of dreams
Glasses of Champagne
Princesses' dresses
Just for one night
A night at the Opera
It's dawn already
I close the book again
I'm going to sleep
And maybe dream again

Above the garden
(*in the diaphanous hours*)

In the wind I'm dropping
Among my sisters of rain
We'll fall friends
On the big glass roof
On the zinc of the gutter
On all that green garden
This frosted glass for the morning light
All that water for those dead leaves
Forgotten since that old fall
We'll sing the hothouses
Their Natural History Museum summers
Their orange trees far from winter
Sheltered from the tears, comforted
Warmed up, sweetened by the sun
Drenched with the sun's water
In the so much hoped for diaphanous hours

Free

I had never read the lyrics
Since 1970
I was 12 years old
"*Poetry hesitates
Between sound and meaning*"
Words don't matter
The little stories
Two couplets
A chorus
A great song
For the guts
For the heart
The message is in the riff
Instant
What's left is for grown-ups
It's Art
With its drawers
Its positions
Its Aesthetic
Its judgements
Its loftiness
Rock doesn't care
Me too
It's free for the ears
During 3 little minutes
"It's all right now…!"
Yeah… It's all right…

The pebble

I'll go to Étretat (*Normandy*)
Certainly
There I'll put it down
On the shore
It'll find the beach again
And its friends
A summer kid
One of those summers so far
Will probably pick it up
My first name in blue
Almost worn away
Salty water
Tides, waves
Time
The old cake box
The treasure box
Ordinary, precious
Shells of holidays
Forgotten things
The nice collection
He's never showing to anyone
In a little girl's eyes
That innocent smile
Under a july sun
Then they will hide
For her he will open
The lid and his heart
He'll let her see wonders

And he'll give to her for life
This pebble, this jewel
Mischievous little flower
She won't say a word to him
She'll understand

A day in the life of John Lennon

The dreamers, the poets
At the funfair
Among beaming kids
Alone in the crowd
In summer
Sideshows
Roller coaster
The circus and its music
A hairy clown
His short-sighted look
Lost in his thoughts
Turned toward an ideal world
Which are fraying into reality
Elusive images
Yet so very existing
In his heart
In the bus
Instinctively, by feeling
In the sunny streets
Of the nice season
Hung on lampposts
Multicoloured balloons
A day in the life of John Lennon
A dream drives out another
It's a food
A wounded child's enthusiasm
A door towards hope
In a closed world

Entangled in its emptiness and fears
Love and music
Peace on Earth
In his old rebel's pockets
Little lad's holding on...!
He wants to imagine everything
Too bad for illusions...!
Too bad for utopias...!
He can imagine everything
Even a better world
A world without wars
Without pains and tears
He has imagined everything
He stuck out his tongue
At all those old stories
Of power and money
Just one tree is enough
Little flower of May
He's already changed everything
It had to be done
And done again
He did his best
He did what he could
He has just imagined
A day in the life of John Lennon

The gardens of the Alhambra

Summer and its nights
Sharing the sweet fruit
Pomegranate tasting like a kiss
Perfume of friendly flowers
And our Spanish lips
In the gardens of the Alhambra
I'll take you in my arms
Andalusian, silently taking flight
I'll go there, by the ways
Until the intimate, the hideaway
This tender discovery
This garden in the gardens
And then dawn slowly
Will come to draw the paths
And the sun will be able to love
The gardens and the lovers

It's five o'clock

As he came out of school
My old French teacher
On his way to the station was humming that song
"It's five o'clock"
Its lyrics are touching
Deep
When we understand English
The voice is powerful
Thick and sweet at the same time
With a greek accent
All radios were playing it
One of my first singles
Haloed by the sun of Athens
Piraeus was pop
Aphrodite's beauty
I wanted dreams
I still want some
A song for happiness
Just a little happiness
It doesn't take that much

An autumn's tale (*one season episode three*)

Epilogue

Time is not for eclogue
Even if fall has its sun
The wind's whispering its monologues
Silently humming to the sky
Prisoner in the Tower of London
The Prince in exile remembers
It's raining, the Thames is so dark
Like that Monet she liked so much
Time is only for antiphons
In the forsaken park
One can hear those ancient songs
Between swaying trees
The Queen of England has reprieved the Prince
"Your sorrow, my Lord, is well worth all of our dungeons!"
A last cup of tea in Buckingham Palace
"Your words, Your Majesty, will ever sound so warm to me!"
During the crossing, he's staring at the Channel
His landau stowed among the cars
A stormy sea, no ball, no dance
On the deck of the ferry
Soon the day will come
Echoes of music in his sleepy Palace
Those faraway waltzs which coloured the time
And that old Captain so British
Told him on the dock
"Please, wait for springtime my Lord!"

An Englishman

An Englishman so far from home
On the "*Promenade des Anglais*"
White jacket
Spring
Staring at the hill
A flower between his lips
It's sunset
He's silently living
The fool
He's so handsome
Simply
Loving
Day after day
So nice in Nice

December

Snow on the wood
A rain of cold ashes
December goes away
Dawn after dawn
Its sad and wandering days
It's snowing silence
Snowflakes of voiceless tears
On the cheeks of absence
And December's standing still
Gazing upon the wood
Then turns its head away
Yes… December moves away
Its frozen steps, its festive atmospheres
It's snowing in the house
Those shadowy sundays
Which capsize and then sink
In the evenings
Without horizon
Snow in my heart
As sorrow Decembers
All the minutes, all the colours
Last embers soon to be ashes

Hard day's clouds

Veiled
Sun
Unveiled
Atmospheric alternation
A hesitating sky
Hard day's clouds
Four of them in my mind
Between grey and white
On this blue springtime
On the garden
On the plants
On the new flowers
On the roofs of old buildings
A forgotten storm
Plants already are splashing about
Perfumes, scents
For the daytime's walkers
It's been raining
On the trees
On the paths
All the leaves
Generous and green
I'm coming back in here
The benches are dry
Poems in light
Rimbaud after the downpour
Nice weather on the grass
Soon summer

Birds already
On the branches
In flight
Everywhere small creatures are busy
Bundles… Ants
The great club of insects
It's warm in the heart of things
It's all new
It's good like that
It's pretty good

It's falling

It's gently falling
Silent rain
Its tears in the wind
Day and night
It's falling without haste
And relentlessly covers
The chairs, the eyes, the tables
Uniform and greyish
The broom despairs
The dusters resign
It's time which draws
Its shadows under the dust
It's falling on the words
Of these blue poems
Which were dancing
Light and joyful
Full of sentences
Of happy suns
It's falling on the flame
Of that piece of candle
Which enlighted the night
It's even turning off the tears
And the garden is bored
Its lonely strollers
No more flowers in flowerbeds
So dust is falling
On the sleeping trees
Those white sheets on furniture

When the house darkens
To each room its shadow
Its blind and empty heart
It's falling there too
In the abandoned hours
Armchairs, wilted curtains
So far, far from life
Under the dust
Grief

Abba

A sledge and its dogs
In North Sweden
A snow storm
I lost my way
My compass is spinning
The songs of the island
Off Stockolm
Are so far
In the blizzard
They're passing by
Ghost suns
Of these old summers
The game is over
Nobody for the stake
My hands are cold
And the cards are sliding
Between my fingers of winter
Of the polar circle
Not the heart to play
What's left in all this white…?
A glitter ball
A dancing queen
Under the snowflakes
A frozen heart
Which has nothing to win
Which has lost everything
Even its memories of joy
Driven away by avalanches of tears

It has an igloo left
An emergency beacon
And some old disco tunes

Gleam

This hazy gleam
Hardly a sun
Hardly a dawn
A thought which shows through
That the eyes can't see
That no word can say
Maybe a sound
The silence maybe
Hardly a motion
A gesture of the hand
Towards the stars... Afar
Hardly a colour
The flapping of the blue
Of a skimmed sky

The complete works of The Beatles

In Alice's land
Some forgotten wonders
Among brambles
Footsteps in the gravel
Flattened grasses
Too long
Forsaken
Without a gardener
Wild flowers
Don't speak any language
Stubborn to all winds
They don't remind anymore
Though maybe vaguely
Of that english garden
Where formerly blossomed
Songs and dreams
Dazzling the sky
It was another world
In Alice's eyes
The garden is closed
The last memories
The ones which weren't looted
And put in museum
Wander in the old childhoods
Which don't want to end
The ordinary chaos
Can't hear the brass bands anymore
Which walked along the road

And streaked with hopes
All the ways of sun and rain
On a bench, under the leaves
It seems to be a guitar
Branches intertwined
It seems to be a neck
Strings
Suffice to believe it
To see it
At night it's playing
The complete works of The Beatles

www.ingramcontent.com/pod-product-compliance
Lightning Source LLC
LaVergne TN
LVHW041546070426
835507LV00011B/949